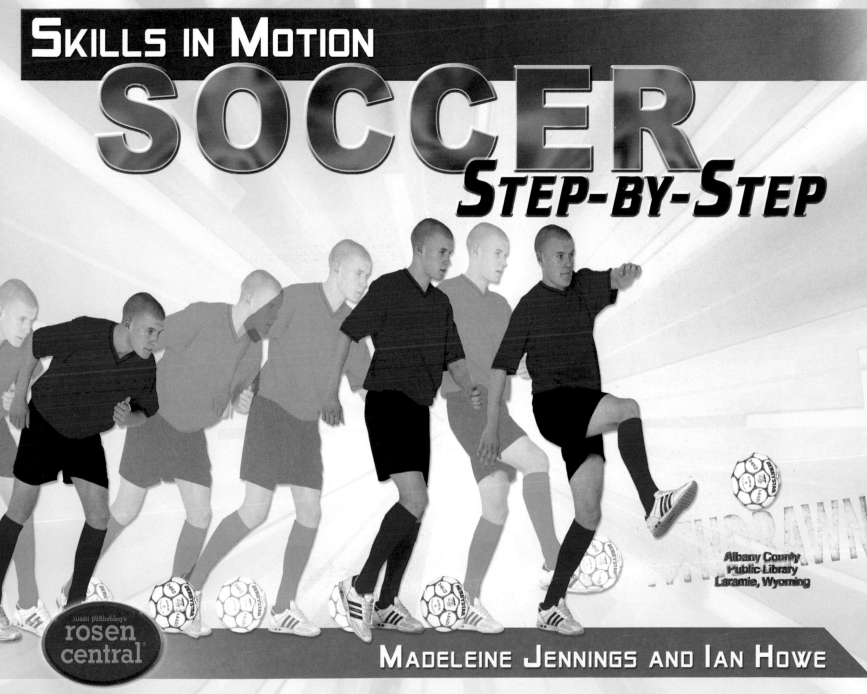

SKILLS IN MOTION

SOCCER

STEP-BY-STEP

rosen central

New York

MADELEINE JENNINGS AND IAN HOWE

This edition published in 2010 by:

The Rosen Publishing Group, Inc.
29 East 21st Street
New York, NY 10010

Library of Congress Cataloging-in-Publication

Jennings, Madeleine.
Soccer step-by-step / Madeleine Jennings and Ian Howe.
    p. cm.—(Skills in motion)
Includes bibliographical references and index.
ISBN-13: 978-1-4358-3362-3 (library binding)
1. Soccer—Handbooks, manuals, etc. I. Howe, Ian, 1962– II. Title.
GV943.J393 2009
796.334—dc22

                          2009012538

Manufactured in the United States of America

CPSIA Compliance Information: Batch #BR902021YA: For Further Information contact Rosen Publishing, New York, New York at 1-800-237-9932.

contents

introduction

SOCCER is one of the most popular team sports in the world. The spread of both the men's and women's game has been helped hugely by the amount of media coverage given to the sport, with professional games from all over the world transmitted to all households with a television.

Every soccer skill seen on our televisions started somewhere: a practice field, playground, local park, or even a clumsy first attempt in the backyard. People play sports for a variety of reasons, ranging from fun, competition, a way of keeping fit, or purely as a social activity where they can meet new friends. All sports provide enjoyment, fitness, and the learning of new skills, which, in most cases, are different from the skills used in everyday life.

Whatever the individual reason for taking up soccer, there is always room for improvement. Professional and amateur players are constantly striving to enhance their abilities on the field, and this requires a well-balanced training program. For years, ordinary coaching manuals using ordinary photographs failed to show the key point of every movement. By studying the sequence of photographs in this book and copying the body shapes and foot movements, you can easily enhance your skills and develop new ones.

WARMING UP Always warm up before a training session to get the blood pumping throughout your body and to help prevent injuries. Try lifting one leg at a time and lightly touching the top of a stationery ball with the soles of your shoes (left) or keeping on your toes while passing the ball between your feet (far left).

what is a skill?

By definition, a soccer skill is a series of interlinked moves that requires special ability or expertise. It also requires special training. There is a beginning, middle, and end to each skill, and these can be practiced individually, then put together and practiced in their entirety.

Learning skills should be fun, so do not work on one exercise for more than 15 minutes at a time. Always move onto a new activity before you tire of the old one. An entire skills training session should not exceed 1 hour for players under 13 years of age.

This book concentrates on the following basic skills:

1. CONTROLLING
2. PASSING
3. DRIBBLING
4. TURNING
5. SHOOTING
6. HEADING
7. GOALKEEPING

As the game becomes more competitive, technical, and physical, all players—regardless of their position on the field —require a broader range of skills. Defenders need to learn

how to receive the ball at any height or angle, bring it under control, and progress play, just as strikers need to learn defensive moves. So, aim to make learning new skills an enjoyable part of training sessions.

putting skills into practice

Once you have become familiar and competent with each of the different soccer skills, you need to learn when to use them. Do not use a complicated skill when there is a simpler alternative.

Before you even come into contact with the ball, you need to ask yourself questions: Am I in danger of losing the ball? Do I need to use a defensive skill? Are there teammates nearby? Can I pass the ball? Is the path clear to run with the ball? Can I aim for the goal? Deciding what skill to use when is what makes a good player.

practice makes perfect

With quality practice sessions, you should see improvements in your skills within a six-month period. Monitor your skills and fitness level on a simple chart (see opposite). For instance, if you are practicing turns, time yourself for one minute over 5 yards (4.5 meters) to see how many you can make. Record the result and check in a week's time over the same distance for the same amount of time. If you do just one more, you know you are improving.

START OFF SLOW Always start each section of a training skill at a walking pace. Pay specific attention to your body shape and the part of the foot (contact surface) you need to use to play the ball. As you become more confident and comfortable with the moves, you can pick up the pace.

KEEPING RECORDS

SKILL	THE CHALLENGE	DURATION	DATE / SCORE	DATE / SCORE	DATE / SCORE	DATE / SCORE
turns	turn between two cones 5 yd (4.5 m) apart	1 minute	1/1/10 10	1/8/10 11	1/15/10 12	1/22/10 11
passing	working with a friend passing through cones 10 yd (9 m) apart	1 minute	1/1/10 20	1/18/10 22		
heading						
shooting						
dribbling						

If you are not improving at a particular skill, don't worry. Just go back over it section by section, trying to identify the parts of the skill that you need to improve on, and work on those again. Remember always to set yourself achievable targets—it goes hand in hand with skills improvements.

play safe

Overtraining is just as bad as not training enough. Many young soccer players suffer burnout by playing in too many games, accompanied by excessive training over a short period. You should always rest between games and training sessions to achieve your maximum level of performance. Other things to bear in mind include wearing the appropriate protective clothing (see pp. 8–9). You should not practice if conditions are wet, or if you are not feeling well or are tired or injured. Always wait until you have fully recovered; otherwise, you may cause a long-term repetitive injury.

ball trajectories

Experiment with the ball and you will find that you can create different movements by striking the ball at different angles with different parts of the foot. For example, striking the right side of the ball with the inside of your right foot will bend the ball left. Striking the left side of the ball with the outside of your right foot will bend the ball right. And striking the ball underneath will send it spiraling up.

equipment

footwear

Wearing the appropriate training shoes is very important when practicing soccer skills. Different surfaces and weather conditions call for different kinds of footwear. Choosing the right one will help you maximize your skills and avoid any injuries.

Choose soccer footwear for comfort and safety, not for color or any other style aspect. Make sure you wear the correct size—wearing ones that don't fit can cause long-term injuries.

A basic pair of sneakers with flat surfaces and a good tread should be worn on concrete and indoor surfaces.

PLAYING ON CONCRETE Wear sneakers that have a flat surface and good tread. If it has been raining, the surface may be slippery, so always check before you start to practice or play a game. Do not practice if puddles are still visible on concrete surfaces.

PLAYING ON SOFT GROUND Wear soccer cleats with changeable cleats. Keep an eye out for uneven wear of cleats and immediately replace any that become sharp on an edge. A new blade system of shoes can also be worn on soft ground. Always keep footwear clean in between games because sloppiness can reflect on your performance.

AstroTurf cleats are good to wear when playing on hard ground.

PLAYING ON GRASS In the summer when playing fields become hard, wear sturdy cleats.

the ball

Always make sure the ball you choose is not too big or heavy for the players. Below is a recommended guideline.

UNDER **9** YEARS OF AGE	SIZE **3**
9 TO **14** YEARS OF AGE	SIZE **4**
OVER **14** YEARS OF AGE	SIZE **5**

shin pads

These should be worn during all games and practices whenever there is contact between two players. It is illegal to play in games without shin pads, and players will be disqualified for failure to do so. Some pads slip down behind the sock, but others with ankle protectors need to be put on before socks. Choose your pads wisely for comfort and maximum protection.

markers

You can buy simple markers from sports retailers, but any suitable object can be used to set up working grids for training.

For obvious safety reasons, never use sharp or fragile objects as markers.

goalkeeper's outfit

In addition to shin pads, goalkeepers also have the option of wearing shirts and shorts with built-in padding. This helps to soften the impact when they dive toward a ball.

Goalkeeping gloves come in many different varieties and vary hugely in price. Choose a pair that fit well and tighten around the wrist, which prevents them from falling off. They should have good grip on the palms where they come into contact with the ball. Some gloves now have reinforced fingers for added protection, but they are much more expensive than normal ones.

Shin pads are an essential part of your soccer equipment.

stretching

Always warm up your muscles with 10 minutes of stretching before a training session. Equally important is a cooling-down stretch session once you have finished. Stretching has the following benefits. It:

- Prepares the body for activity, signaling to your brain that your muscles are about to be used.
- Reduces muscle tension by making the body more relaxed.
- Improves coordination and increases range of motion.
- Prevents muscle strains (a strong, prestretched muscle resists stress better than a strong, unstretched muscle) and repetitive injuries.
- Helps to create body awareness.
- Promotes circulation.

Twisting from side to side with your feet planted on the ground will stretch your hips and lower back.

Bending forward with your weight on your front leg will stretch your calf muscles.

Leaning forward to touch your toes will stretch your hamstring muscles.

Practice with a partner by standing back to back and passing the ball. This will stretch your hips.

go with the flow

Flowmotion is a revolutionary photographic coaching system. In a series of detailed photographs, it shows every movement and body shape used in basic soccer skills and not just the selected highlights. This enables readers to teach themselves with far more accuracy, without the presence of a coach. Just by following the step-by-step Flowmotion pages, you can improve and learn new skills in your own time. The captions along the bottom of the images provide additional information to help you perform the skills confidently. Below this, another layer of information includes basic instructions and symbols indicating when to move forward. On pages 78, 79, 82, and 83, the blue marker represents the player's opponent.

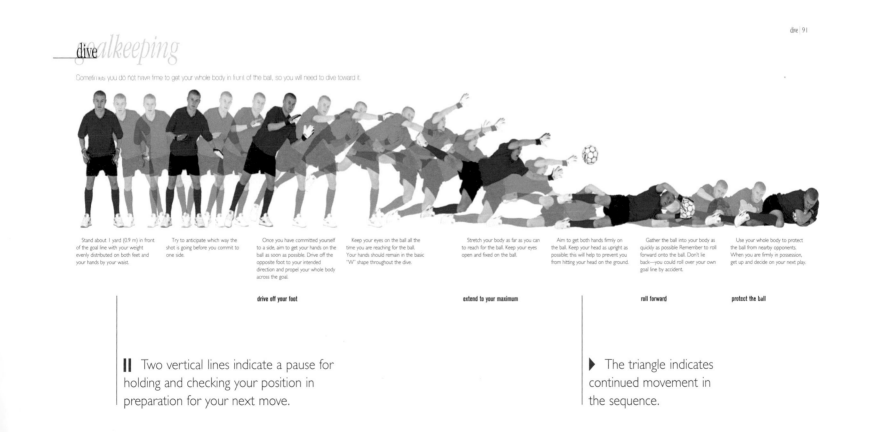

dive | 91

goalkeeping
dive

Sometimes you do not have time to get your whole body in front of the ball, so you will need to dive toward it.

Stand about 1 yard (0.9 m) in front of the goal line with your weight evenly distributed on both feet and your hands by your waist.

Try to anticipate which way the shot is going before you commit to one side.

Once you have committed yourself to a side, aim to get your hands on the ball as soon as possible. Drive off the opposite foot to your intended direction and propel your whole body across the goal.

Keep your eyes on the ball all the time you are reaching for the ball. Your hands should remain in the basic "W" shape throughout the dive.

Stretch your body as far as you can to reach for the ball. Keep your eyes open and fixed on the ball.

Aim to get both hands firmly on the ball. Keep your head as upright as possible; this will help to prevent you from hitting your head on the ground.

Gather the ball into your body as quickly as possible. Remember to roll forward onto the ball. Don't lie back—you could roll over your own goal line by accident.

Use your whole body to protect the ball from nearby opponents. When you are firmly in possession, get up and decide on your next play.

drive off your foot

extend to your maximum

roll forward

protect the ball

‖ Two vertical lines indicate a pause for holding and checking your position in preparation for your next move.

▶ The triangle indicates continued movement in the sequence.

passing

control and side foot pass

passing

The aim of this maneuver is to receive the ball from another player, bring it under control, then pass it on again. The inside of your foot offers the widest surface to make contact with the ball, so pass with this part because it will give you more accuracy. Note that this player is left-footed.

● Keep a close eye on the ball as it comes toward you. Keep your arms out to your sides, away from your body, for good balance.

● Start to swing your arms as you run to the right side of the ball. Then sidestep to the left of it. Getting your body to the line of the ball is crucial.

● You may need to sidestep twice before you are in the correct position. Stay on your toes all the while, which will help you keep your balance.

approach ▶ **sidestep** ▶

● Once you are in the right position, plant your leg firmly to a stop; then turn your left leg out so you stop the ball with your inside left foot.

● When you have got the ball under control, step back with your left leg to get ready for the outward pass.

● Use your arms to give your body the momentum it needs to carry through with the pass.

● Aim to pass the ball back in the direction it came from with your left foot. Practice this skill with both feet, so you can improve on your least favorite foot.

make contact ❙❙ ▶ ▶ **follow through** ❙❙

control and outside foot pass

passing

This is similar to the side foot pass, but instead of using the inside of your foot to pass the ball, you need to use the outside part of your foot. When practicing with a partner, try to keep the ball low to make control easier.

● Face sideways as you start your run toward the oncoming ball. Just before you reach it, sidestep to your left to get in line with the ball.

● Your touch on the ball should place it in front of you. You will now be able to step into the next part of the pass and the ball will not be stuck underneath your feet.

● Put your right foot all the way down; then take a step forward with your left foot.

● Aim to strike the ball with your right foot, which means you need to bring your leg across your body.

● As you lean forward, point your foot slightly to the left of the ball. Once you have struck the ball with the outside of your foot, look up toward your target.

● This type of pass should create some spin on the ball, which will make it curve from left to right.

● Try to maintain your composure, and keep your upper body loose and relaxed as you follow through with the kick.

II   **kick**   ▶   ▶   **follow through**   II

control and change feet

passing

To avoid an oncoming defender, you need to be able to change the direction of the ball's play. To do this, practice receiving the ball with one foot, then passing it on with the other. Changing feet becomes very important once you start dribbling the ball.

● Try to get up on your toes as you step up to the oncoming ball. Don't take your eye off the ball. As the ball approaches, decide which foot you want to control it with to take it in the direction you want.

● Once the ball is in easy reach, plant your right foot down and stretch out with your left leg. Turn your left toes out to catch the ball on the inside of your left foot.

● Bring the ball under control; then take your left leg forward, placing the foot down slightly across your body.

● To change direction, turn your shoulders to the right. Keep your eye on the ball as you do so.

● Pick up your right leg and turn the toes out so you can kick the ball with the inside of your right foot.

● Look toward your pass and then back to the ball as you move to kick it. Strike the ball with the side of your foot for accuracy.

● Don't forget to use your upper body as you follow through with the kick as smoothly as possible.

change direction ❚❚ ▶ ▶ **follow through** ❚❚

lofted pass

Getting height on a stationary ball is useful when you need to pass it into attacking areas, with the aim of scoring a header into the goal. It's also good for long-distance passing.

● When striking a dead (motionless) ball, look at your intended target; then begin to approach the ball.

● Gauge the distance between yourself and the ball as you run toward it. Swing your arms to give you some momentum and balance.

● Once you are close enough, look back down as you address the ball. Aim to get your non-kicking foot beside the ball.

● As you approach the ball, take your right leg back and prepare to make the loft kick. Begin to lean back.

● Keep your eye on the ball as you use the instep of your right foot to strike the underside of the ball.

● Lean back with your upper body to give your kick more power and the ball more loft. Lift your arms up and out to your sides to help with balance.

● Follow through by bending your left knee as you raise your right foot and leg as high as possible. This will help give the ball height.

distance throwing in

To achieve a long-distance throw, hold the ball high above your head, keeping your elbows straight. This will allow you to harness the power in your shoulders and throw the ball a greater distance. Try to make the throw a continous, smooth action. Keep your feet behind the line and both hands on the ball.

● Use both hands to hold the ball firmly out in front of you. Look toward your intended target.

● Take a step forward toward the throwing-in line with your left leg as you raise the ball above your head.

● Take another step in with your right leg; then brace your arms and bring them as far back as possible behind your head to create a catapult effect.

● When you bring your arms forward again, the whole of the back and upper body should create an elastic effect to power the ball as it uncoils and straightens.

● Use your back foot to give your throw added power. Release the ball when it is at head height.

● Follow through by bending forward with your upper body and bringing your arms down to your side. Make sure both feet are still behind the line.

● The strength and distance of the throw will be determined by the run up and the arch of your back. Keep both feet on the ground.

II   **release the ball**   **II**

control

chest control

To bring a high, incoming ball under control, use your chest. Rather than presenting a completely rigid surface to the ball, let your body give a bit as the ball makes contact. This way you'll have greater control over the ball when it drops down to your feet.

- As you follow the incoming ball with your eyes, keep your body alert by bending your knees and elbows.

- Lean back, keep your arms clear of the ball, and stick out your chest in preparation for the arrival of the ball.

- Ease your chest back when the ball makes contact. This will help to cushion the ball and give you greater control. The ball should drop to the ground in front of you.

● Bring your left foot forward for stability as you pick up your right foot in preparation for the kick.

● Keep your eyes on the ball as you lean forward and bring your right leg back. Make sure your arms stay out to the side, as this will help with balance.

● Use the right side of your foot to pass the ball on. This is the widest surface you can hit the ball with, so it will make your pass more accurate.

● Raise your right leg high, and lean back slightly to follow through with the pass-through. Keep your rhythm smooth as you do so.

gain control ▶ kick ▶ follow through Ⅱ

head control

Many beginners avoid heading the ball because they are worried it will hurt. However, if you do the move properly, using the correct part of your head, it won't. The key is to absorb the energy of the ball by easing back a fraction when the ball makes contact. Then, when the ball drops down to the ground, it won't bounce away. Only practice heading balls for short periods of time.

● Once you have moved into position to receive the ball, step back onto your right foot. Keep your elbows bent with your hands up by your chest.

● As the ball comes toward you, lean back. Keep your eyes open and focused on the ball.

● Aim to make contact with your forehead. As the ball arrives, lean farther back so your forehead absorbs the energy of the ball through the neck muscles.

● Direct the ball to your side by moving your head down toward your feet. Keep your eyes fixed on the ball.

● Use your right foot to get the ball under control; then prepare to pass the ball with the inside of your right foot.

● Place your left foot alongside the ball, pointing in the direction of the kick. Swing back your right leg so you can bring the inside of your right foot in contact with the ball. Follow through with a smooth, flowing motion.

make contact ▶ ▶ **prepare to pass** ▶ **follow through** II

thigh control

The key to receiving the ball on your thigh is to keep your entire body supple and relaxed. When the ball comes into contact with your thigh, draw the leg away slightly so you soften its impact. Do not make the mistake of hitting the ball with your knee, as this will cause it to bounce away, out of control.

● Stand with your feet hip width apart and knees slightly bent in readiness for the oncoming ball.

● Keep your eye on the ball as you follow its path down toward you. Begin to lift up your right knee.

● By the time the ball makes contact, your thigh should be raised at a 45-degree angle to your body.

track the ball || **raise knee** || **make contact**   ▶

● Once the ball makes contact, lower your thigh slightly to cushion the impact. Use your thigh to guide the ball down in front of you and to your left.

● As you bring the ball under your control, step in and turn toward your left. Lean forward and bring your right leg back as you prepare to pass.

● Your left foot should be positioned alongside the ball, pointing in the direction you are aiming toward.

● Kick the ball with the inside of your right foot. Follow through by leaning back and looking up.

▶ step in ▶ pass the ball ▶ ‖

side foot control

To gain control of a high, lofted pass, you will most likely need to use both feet to settle the ball down onto the ground. Most players prefer to use one foot more than the other, but you should try to develop the weaker foot because it will be useful when you are learning to dribble the ball.

● As you prepare for the oncoming ball, make sure your body is relaxed and you are up on your toes.

● As the ball comes toward you, step forward onto your left foot. Hold your arms out to your sides to give you greater balance.

● Raise your right knee and turn your toes out so the inside of your right foot faces toward the ball. Step on the ball to control it.

● The ball will most likely bounce a bit toward your left. Transfer your weight from left to right so you can pick up your left foot and use it to bring the ball back to the center, between your feet.

● Step up to the ball with your left foot, ready to kick with your right. Your left foot should be beside the ball, with your toes pointing in the direction of your aim.

● As you prepare to kick, bring your right shoulder and leg back. This will help give you a good swing so you can get some height on the ball.

● Focus on the ball as you use the inside of your right foot to kick it. Hold your arms out wide as you follow through with the kick.

shooting

dead ball shoot

This technique is good for producing an accurate and powerful shot for a target a long distance away.

● You'll need to keep your eye on the ball once you begin the shot, so start by fixing a target in your mind's eye.

● Keep your gaze on the ball as you begin to step up to it. Swing your arms to give you momentum.

● Step up with your left leg so your left foot lies right up alongside, or even slightly in front of, the ball.

● As you bring your right foot in to make the kick, lean slightly over to the left and trail your right shoulder. This will give you more room to swing and therefore more power behind the ball.

● Try to strike the ball with the front of your boot so your laces make contact with the ball.

● To create curl and swerve, approach the ball from right to left, rather than straight on. Striking different sections of the ball will produce different flight movements.

● Follow through with the kick by bringing your foot right up to waist height. Look up and swing with your arms to give the kick more momentum. For more power, jump off your left, non-kicking foot.

▶ **make contact** ▶ **II follow through**

left side volley

The volley is the most powerful way to kick the ball, and requires not only strength but also precision, timing, and balance. It's a great ball skill to have, especially if you need to shoot a goal with the ball approaching at waist height. This sequence shows a left-footed player, but you should always practice with your weaker side, as well as your preferred side.

● As the ball approaches, keep your eyes firmly fixed on it. You need to strike across the direction of the oncoming ball.

● If you use your left foot to kick the ball, lean away with your right shoulder as you step up for the shot. This will allow your striking foot to swing across your body at knee height.

● Pivot on the ball of your right foot as you take take the shot with your left. Keep your left arm out to provide good balance.

‖ watch the ball   approach   ▶   kick   ▶

● As you strike the ball with the instep (or laces), your whole body should swing across to the right to give the ball its momentum. To complete the follow-through, step all the way around onto your left foot.

● You can practice this skill with a partner, who throws a ball toward you. Remember to swap positions after a couple of tries.

● If you are throwing the ball in, keep both feet firmly planted on the ground, bend your knees, and hold the ball with both hands.

straight volley

A straight volley involves kicking the ball back in the same direction as it arrived. It is often used when the ball has been cleared by a goalie or defender. Do not lean back; this will cause the ball to rise too high.

● Watch the ball as it comes in your direction. You need to get well behind the ball, so adjust your position accordingly.

● As you step up to the ball, put your arms out to the sides to help you keep your balance.

● Keep your eyes fixed on the ball as you swing your right arm back and raise your right knee up high. You should hit the ball with the front of your foot so that your laces make contact with it.

● Keep the angle of your kicking foot slight so you create a smooth, straight path with the ball. Follow through by raising your kicking leg high and then stepping forward onto it.

● If you are throwing the ball in, keep both feet firmly planted on the ground, bend your knees, and hold the ball with both hands.

● You can also throw the ball underarm to your partner. Do not make the throw too hard or fast.

shot from side delivery

Receiving the ball from a side-on pass and then shooting with just one touch requires a lot of skill. The key is timing your steps and the shot with the arrival of the ball. It may seem tricky, but with practice, it is definitely achievable. Note that this player is left-footed. If you are right-footed, simply switch the feet instructions.

● Timing is crucial for this maneuver, so you need to watch the ball closely as it comes all the way into your feet.

● As the ball comes close, step up with your non-kicking leg (in this case, your right leg).

● Allow the ball to come across your right foot before it comes into contact with your left foot.

● Keep your eyes firmly on the ball, your arms out to the sides, and elbows behind you as you aim to shoot with one touch.

● Bring your right shoulder forward and your left arm back as you put some momentum into the kick.

● Aim to strike the ball slightly across your body. Once you have kicked the ball, follow through by stepping forward onto your left foot.

● As you steady yourself, look up to see if the ball has reached its intended target. This shot is difficult to achieve at first, but gets easier with practice.

make contact ▶ ❚❚ ▶ ❚❚

getting past opponents

step over/half scissors

This technique allows you to bypass your defender by putting him or her off balance. You need to have good ball control and be able to dribble quickly from side to side. Performing this at the right distance from the opponent is crucial: too far away and it will be ineffective; too close and you will get tackled.

● Crouch over the ball, keeping your arms slightly out to the sides to protect the ball from other defenders.

● When you are about 1 to 1½ yards (0.9-1.4 m) in front of the defender, begin the move. If you are too close, you will be tackled; and if you are too far, the move will not be effective.

● Get down low and bend your left knee as you make an exaggerated move toward your left.

protect the ball ▶   ▶ fake to left ▶

● To fake the leftward movement, you need to step over the ball, rather than kick it, and quickly power to the other side.

● Use the toes of your right foot to push the ball to the right of the defender; then follow on toward your right side.

● By doing this, you will hopefully have thrown the defender off balance. Before he or she can regain equilibrium, you can move forward with the ball.

● Once you have passed the defender, accelerate away and make a pass or shoot at the goal.

▶ **move to the right** ▶ **bypass defender** ▶ **pass the ball on** ‖

shoulder drop

The aim of this maneuver is to throw your opponent off balance. By dipping your shoulder, you are encouraging him or her to lean over one way. You, however, change direction by moving the ball with the outside of your foot. This is a left-footed sequence.

● Keep your eye on the path in front of you as you nudge the ball forward with your left foot.

● Alternate your focus between the ball and the defender as you continue dribbling the ball forward, gathering speed.

● When you are about 1 yard (0.9 m) away from your opponent, begin the move by stepping onto your right foot.

edge forward ▶ step onto right foot ▶

● As you shift your body weight onto your right leg, dip your right shoulder. This will encourage your opponent to also lean to the right in an attempt to tackle you. The more exaggerated the dip, the more effective you will be.

● When your opponent moves to the right, you should quickly change direction to the left.

● As you nudge the ball to the left, your opponent will be struggling to regain his or her balance.

● You should now be past your opponent, in full possession and control of the ball. Accelerate away and pass or shoot at the goal.

move toward the right ▶ **change direction** ▶   ▶   ‖

roll over

This is another way of outwitting your opponent and getting the ball past him or her. It involves moving the ball quickly from side to side, creating sudden changes of direction to your path.

● Keep your eye on the ball and your arms out to your sides, which will help you maintain your balance.

● Continue focusing on the ball as you use the outside of your right foot to edge the ball slowly forward.

● Lean toward your left side and reach out with your right foot so it is resting on the ball's outer surface.

❚❚ ▶ **move forward** ▶ **reach out to far side of ball** ❚❚

● Continue leaning to your left as you roll your foot over the ball. You should roll the ball with the base of your foot so it moves from right to left.

● This sudden rolling moving will fool your opponent, who has moved to your left in the expectation that you will play the ball on this side.

● Once you have rolled the ball to your left, lean forward as you play the ball with your left foot.

● You should be clear of any defense now and able to play the ball to the left of your previous defender and accelerate away.

step over

Another way of beating a player is to transfer your body weight from left to right (or vice versa) and step over the ball. This gives the illusion that you are going to play the ball with one foot, but you actually step over the ball and use your other foot instead.

● Push the ball forward with your right foot. Crouch over the ball as you stay low to the ground.

● Keep your eye on the ball, looking up every now and then to check your opponent's position on the field.

● Move your left leg toward the ball as if you are intending to kick it with your left foot. Instead, take your left leg over the ball.

stay low ▶ ▶ **fool your opponent** ▶

● Once your left foot is over the ball and firmly planted on the ground, transfer your body weight and play the ball with your right foot.

● With the defender fooled and off balance, you are now free to take the ball off and around the defender.

● Play the ball away from the defender with your right foot. Stay low to the ground.

● Keep your eyes firmly fixed on the ball as you knock the ball into a good stride pattern.

turns

stop turn

This is the best turn to use when you have a defender running alongside you and you want to shake him or her off by changing your direction suddenly.

● Keep your eyes on the ball as you dribble it forward, maintaining close control over it. Look up every few strides to check your position.

● As your opponent draws close to you, keep him or her guessing as to what you are planning to do.

● Put your leading right foot on top of the ball to stop it suddenly. Use your momentum to step over the stationary ball.

● Plant your right foot in front of the ball, then pivot on it as you bring your left leg around in a clockwise direction.

● You should be turning your body so your back is facing toward your opponent. Lean back in toward him or her.

● Regain your balance as you push off the left foot, and use the right foot to dribble the ball forward.

● As you accelerate in the opposite direction, your opponent will, hopefully, still be moving in the original direction of play.

turn around ▶ **dribble in the opposite direction** ◀

This maneuver is similar to the stop turn, but has the added advantage of pushing the ball back in the opposite direction before you turn around, giving you a head start.

● As you dribble the ball forward, take your arms out to your sides to help you maintain your balance.

● Stay firmly focused on the ball as you continue nudging it forward. Look up every now and then to check your position. Try to keep the defender guessing as to what your next move will be.

● When you have touched the ball forward with your left foot, bring the right foot over the ball.

● Make contact with the ball by placing your right foot on the ball. Make sure the heel of your right foot is touching its surface.

● Your left foot should be firmly planted on the ground as you lean forward, and drag the ball back with the sole of your foot, working from heel to toe.

● Put the right foot back down onto the ground, then pivot on the ball of your right foot as you turn around in a clockwise direction.

● Once you are facing in the opposite direction, drive off the left foot to accelerate and follow the ball.

cruyff turn

This turn relies on you fooling your defender into thinking you are going forward when, in fact, you are making a quick about-face maneuver in the opposite direction.

● Keep your focus on the ball and your arms out to your sides as you dribble the ball forward.

● Crouch down low, making sure your shoulders are well over the ball to protect it from any tackles.

● Gather speed while keeping control over the ball. About 1 yard (0.9 m) in front of your opponent, touch the ball forward with your left foot and pretend to kick the ball with your right.

● Instead of kicking the ball, use the toes to hook the ball and pull it around in the opposite direction.

● Lean toward your left as you pull. Your right leg pulls the ball in toward your left side.

● Swivel on your left foot as you turn your shoulders and then your whole body counterclockwise to the left.

● Push off with your left foot as you lean forward over the ball and accelerate in the opposite direction.

outside hook

This turn is used when you need to make a direction change because there is an opposing player tracking you on your inside. It involves taking the ball back in the opposite direction by keeping your body between the ball and the opponent.

● As you nudge the ball forward, keep your arms out toward your sides and your gaze firmly on the ball.

● Once you have dribbled the ball with your right foot, place the right foot down behind the ball.

● Keeping your eyes on the ball, place your left foot on the left side of the ball; then start to bring your right foot around to the left of the ball.

● Transfer your weight onto your left leg as you lean over to your left side to help you maneuver your foot around the ball.

● Use the outside of your right foot to hook behind the ball, and flick it in the opposite direction.

● Once you have flicked the ball back, follow through by pivoting on the left foot and stepping your right foot around in a clockwise direction.

● Lean forward and drive off the left foot as you propel yourself in the other direction. Use your arms to help you gain some momentum and accelerate away.

inside hook

This turn should be used when you need to change direction because an opponent is on your outside. It involves taking the ball in the opposite direction by keeping your body between the ball and your opponent.

● Keep your eyes fixed on the ball and your hands out to your sides as you nudge the ball forward.

● Dip your left shoulder slightly as you lean to the left, and dribble the ball with your right foot.

● Then, place your right foot behind and to the right of the ball. Keep your eyes fixed on the ball.

move forward ▶ lean to the left ▶ ▶

● Place the left foot beside the ball and to the right. This move should happen quickly so it comes as a surprise to your opponent.

● Lean toward your left as you turn your body in a counterclockwise direction around the ball.

● Use the inside of your right foot to hook the ball, and kick it back in the opposite direction to its original path.

● Look up to check whether your path is clear, and accelerate off your left foot as you move back in the opposite direction.

▶ **hook the ball** ❚❚ ◀

heading the ball

power header

To get power behind a header, you need to use the whole of your upper body, particularly your neck muscles. Don't forget to arch your back and thrust your shoulders forward as you reach for the ball.

● Rock forward onto your left foot a couple of times as you build up momentum for the header.

● As the ball approaches, judge its distance so you can time your rocking with its arrival. You are aiming to strike the ball with your forehead.

● Keep your eyes open and begin to arch your body forward to meet the ball. Aim your forehead at the middle of the ball.

gather momentum ▶   ‖   keep your eyes open ▶

● Once the ball makes contact with your forehead, arch your back and use the whole of your upper body to power it forward. Aim the ball toward your partner's chest.

● Take turns throwing the ball and heading it. Do not do more than 20 headers at one time.

● Throwing the ball underarm will provide a more accurate aim. Make sure you bend your knees and throw the ball with both hands.

make contact

◀ **throw the ball in**

defensive header

These are used to defend

corners and free kicks by

aiming to head the ball away

in a direction opposite to

which it arrived. Heading the

bottom of the ball gives height

to defensive clearance.

● To succeed with a defensive header, it's important to attack the ball to get maximum distance on your header.

● To prepare for the header, rock back and forth, bending down at your knees so they act as a launch pad.

● Judge your timing so you power up to the ball just as it is coming toward you. Aim to hit the bottom of the ball with your forehead.

● As you make contact, extend your neck away from your shoulders to send the ball far and high.

● Aim to get some height on the ball by looping it to your partner so he or she can catch it above his or her head.

● The thrower should always be facing toward the sun. Keep your knees bent and use both hands to throw the ball.

make contact ▶

◀ **throw the ball in**

downward header

The downward header is a good technique to use when you are heading for the goal.

● Keep your eyes fixed on the ball as it comes toward you. You need to time your move to reach the ball at just the right time.

● Rock back onto your right foot to create a launch pad for your header. You can do this a few times to develop greater momentum.

● Use your arms for leverage as you launch yourself forward. Aim to get your forehead above the ball. Plant both feet firmly on the ground to provide a solid base from which to make your header.

● Tilt yourself forward to get above the ball; then tilt your head down so your forehead connects to the top of the ball.

● Add some power to the header by following through with the upper body. Tilt your head down so the ball heads toward the ground.

● If you stand with your feet apart, you can ask your partner to aim the header between your feet.

make contact ▶ **follow through** ❚❚ ◀

jumping header

When competing for an oncoming high ball, you will need to leap up high to get your head to the ball first. Try to get a good running start, and use your whole body— bending your knees and elbows, and arching your upper back—to get the height you require.

● Keep your eyes on the ball as you take a run up toward it. Bend your knees as you run toward it.

● Bend your elbows to use your arms for extra leverage as you jump up toward the ball.

● Bring your head back as you aim to strike the ball with your forehead. Keep your eyes open the whole time.

▶ jump up ▶ strike the ball ▶

● To give your header some power, arch your back when you make contact with the ball. Make sure to bend your knees to cushion your return to the ground.

● If you stand farther back than usual, you will be able to throw the ball higher than normal. This will allow your partner to run up for the header.

● Throw the ball underarm to get more accuracy. Bend your knees and use both hands.

follow through

running with the ball

running short distances with the ball

Dribbling the ball short distances is an important skill to master. You need to keep your eyes on the ball, but at the same time, be aware of your surrounding defenders and the route you aim to take.

● Keep your body crouched low over the ball, with your arms out to the sides. Focus on the ball.

● Begin to move the ball forward by tapping it firmly with the outside of your foot.

● Next, use the inside of your foot to propel the ball farther forward and keep it on track.

stay low ▶ move the ball forward ▶

● Keep your eyes firmly fixed on the ball, but try to maintain an awareness of who and what is around you.

● Try to keep the ball no more than 12–16 inches (0.3–0.4 m) away from you. Any farther and you may quickly lose control over it.

● As you continue to tap the ball with the inside and outside of both feet, dip your shoulders and bend your knees to help you shift your weight from side to side.

● When you become more confident at dribbling the ball, quicken your pace. As you build up speed, you can lift your head up to see around you.

develop pace ▶ **shift your weight** ▶ **11**

running long distances with the ball

Knowing when to run with the ball and when to pass it is what makes a good soccer player. Running a long distance requires only a few touches of the ball. In addition to pace, you will need good control of the ball. Look up occasionally to avoid tackles and assess the situation.

● Start by focusing your eyes firmly on the ball in front of you. Try to keep your shoulders over the ball and your arms out to your sides to protect it from defenders.

● Push the ball forward a good distance, using either the inside or outside of your foot, depending on your intended path.

● Make sure your first touch of the ball is a good one because this will create the stride pattern for the next touch.

protect the ball ▶ **touch the ball** ▶ ▶

● Accelerate your pace. Bend your elbows and swing your arms back and forth to create momentum.

● Each touch of the ball should push it a good distance to maintain your stride pattern.

● As you touch the ball forward, make sure you look up so you can think about your final pass.

● Do not push the ball too far forward, or you will run the risk of losing control over it.

accelerate   ▶   **shift weight**   ▶   **II**

dribbling with both feet

Most players have a favorite foot with which they prefer to play the ball. But don't neglect developing your weaker foot. Although it is difficult, being able to use both feet is a very useful skill when it comes to warding off defenders while running with the ball.

● Crouch down low to the ground with your shoulders over the ball. Start by tapping the ball forward with your outside right foot.

● Keeping your body over the ball, step in with your left foot, and use the outside part to move the ball along.

● As you shift from side to side, dip your shoulders. This will help you transfer your body weight.

crouch down low ▶ **use left foot** ▶ **shift your weight** ▶

● Step in with your right foot again and use the outside part of the foot to move the ball.

● Keep your arms out by your sides and bent at the elbows to help you with your balance.

● Now use the outside of your left foot again to move the ball. The ball should be moving forward in a shallow zigzag manner.

● To maintain control over the ball, keep your knees bent and your eye firmly focused on the ball.

goalkeeping

basic catch

Standing between the posts in the line of fire is not everyone's idea of fun. But goalkeeping is vital for the game and requires not only bravery, but also agility, sound judgment, and good kicking skills. You should aim to always keep up on your toes and be aware of your position in your goalkeeping area—don't remain on your goal line. Always wear the necessary goalkeeping equipment for games, and try to wear gloves during practice.

● Stand about 1 yard (0.9 m) away from the goal line. Bend your knees and keep your weight evenly distributed over the feet. Bend your elbows and keep your hands out in front of you.

● As the ball comes close, step toward it. Keep your eyes firmly fixed on the ball as you reach up with both hands to catch it.

stand steady ▶ **reach up**

● Spread your palms wide so your hands make a "W" shape. Once you make contact with the ball, tighten your grip so you are holding it firmly.

● Continue to cradle the ball tightly with both hands as you bring it in toward your chest.

● Keep the ball close to you as you step out and turn your head, first to the left and then to the right, as you prepare to pass the ball.

● Once you have looked both ways and found a suitable space, you can either kick the ball or throw it out to one of your players.

grip the ball || **look both ways** ||

catch above head

For a high incoming ball, you will need to adjust your position so you can leap up into the air with your arms outstretched above you.

● Keep your body supple as you prepare yourself for the shot. Bend your knees and elbows, and maintain your focus on the ball.

● Once the ball is in the air, step forward well away from the goal line. You don't want to stumble back with the ball and accidentally cross it.

● Reach up with both your hands, making sure the palms are spread wide apart and are facing the ball.

● Step onto your toes as you stretch your body high into the air. You should be aiming to catch the ball at its highest point.

● Once you have caught the ball, draw it in quickly toward your chest with both hands.

● With the ball safely in your possession, look around for opportunities to pass the ball.

● Take your right shoulder back and bring your left one forward as you prepare to throw the ball out.

❚❚   **draw the ball into your chest**   ▶   ❚❚

dive

Sometimes you do not have time to get your whole body in front of the ball, so you will need to dive toward it.

● Stand about 1 yard (0.9 m) in front of the goal line with your weight evenly distributed on both feet and your hands by your waist.

● Try to anticipate which way the shot is going before you commit to one side.

● Once you have committed yourself to a side, aim to get your hands on the ball as soon as possible. Drive off the opposite foot to your intended direction and propel your whole body across the goal.

● Keep your eyes on the ball all the time you are reaching for the ball. Your hands should remain in the basic "W" shape throughout the dive.

drive off your foot ▶

● Stretch your body as far as you can to reach for the ball. Keep your eyes open and fixed on the ball.

● Aim to get both hands firmly on the ball. Keep your head as upright as possible; this will help to prevent you from hitting your head on the ground.

● Gather the ball into your body as quickly as possible. Remember to roll forward onto the ball. Don't lie back—you could roll over your own goal line by accident.

● Use your whole body to protect the ball from nearby opponents. When you are firmly in possession, get up and decide on your next play.

extend to your maximum ▶ **roll forward** ▶ **protect the ball** ▮▮

American Youth Soccer Organization (AYSO)
AYSO National Support & Training Center
12501 South Isis Avenue
Hawthorne, CA 90250
(800) 872-2976
Web site: http://soccer.org/home.aspx
The AYSO was established in the Los Angeles area in 1964 with nine teams. Today, it has more than 50,000 teams and more than 650,000 players. The AYSO has been the leader in establishing groundbreaking youth soccer programs in the United States.

Fédération Internationale de Football Association (FIFA)
FIFA-Strasse 20
P.O. Box 8044
Zurich, Switzerland
Web site: http://www.fifa.com/index.html
FIFA is an association governed by Swiss law founded in 1904 and based in Zurich. It has 208 member associations and its goal, enshrined in its statutes, is the constant improvement of football (what is known in North America as soccer).

Major League Soccer (MLS)
420 5th Avenue, 7th Floor
New York, NY 10018
(877) 557-3774
Web site: http://www.mlsnet.com
Major League Soccer is the top-flight professional soccer league in the United States. It was founded in 1996, after the country hosted the 1994 FIFA World Cup.

Web Sites
Due to the changing nature of Internet links, Rosen Publishing has developed an online list of Web sites related to the subject of this book. This site is updated regularly. Please use this link to access this list:

http://www.rosenlinks.com/sim/socc

Buckley, James. *Pelé*. New York, NY: DK Children, 2007.

Cline-Rasome, Lesa. *Young Pelé*. New York, NY: Schwartz & Wade, 2007.

Crisfield, Deborah W. *The Everything Kids' Soccer Book. Rules, Techniques, and More About Your Favorite Sport!* (Everything Kids). Avon, MA: Adams Media, 2009.

Dorrance, Anson, and Gloria Averbuch. *The Vision of a Champion: Advice and Inspiration from the World's Most Successful Women's Soccer Coach*. Chelsea, MI: Huron River Press, 2005.

Garland, Jim. *Youth Soccer Drills: 84 Drills for Beginning and Intermediate Players*. Champaign, IL: Human Kinetics Publishers, 2003.

Gifford, Clive. *The Kingfisher Soccer Encyclopedia*. Boston, MA: Kingfisher, 2006.

Gifford, Clive. *Soccer: The Ultimate Guide to the Beautiful Game*. Boston, MA: Kingfisher, 2001.

Goldblatt, David. *The Ball Is Round: A Global History of Soccer*. New York, NY: Riverhead, 2008.

Hamm, Mia. *Go for the Goal: A Champion's Guide to Winning in Soccer and Life*. New York, NY: Harper Paperbacks, 2000.

Hornby, Hugh. *Soccer*. New York, NY: DK Children, 2008.

Hunt, Chris, ed. *The Complete Book of Soccer*. New York, NY: Firefly, 2008.

Koger, Robert. *101 Great Youth Soccer Drills*. New York, NY: McGraw-Hill, 2005.

Pelé and Robert L. Fish. *My Life and the Beautiful Game: The Autobiography of Soccer's Greatest Star*. New York, NY: Skyhorse Publishing, 2007.

Radnedge, Keir. *The Ultimate Encyclopedia of Soccer*. London, England: Carlton Books, 2002.

Shea, Therese. *Soccer Stars*. New York, NY: Children's Press, 2007.

U.S. Soccer Federation and Michael Lewis. *Soccer for Dummies*. New York, NY: Wiley Publishing, Inc., 2000.

index

about the author

Ian Howe is a fully qualified coach in the Football Association (England's governing body for soccer), specializing in the coaching of children aged 5–16. Along with two other coaches, he cofounded the successful Palace Soccer School in the early 1990s. The school has close links with many top soccer league clubs throughout England. His work has taken him to many other countries, including the U.S., where he has acquired many new, valuable training methods and techniques from a wide array of professional coaches.